Profiles of the Presidents

RUTHERFORD B. HAYES

★ ★ ★

Profiles of the Presidents

RUTHERFORD B. HAYES

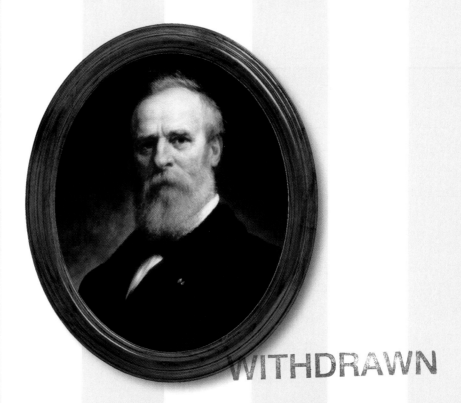

by Andrew Santella

Content Adviser: Roger D. Bridges, Ph.D., Executive Director, The Rutherford B. Hayes Presidential Center, Spiegel Grove, Fremont, Ohio
Reading Adviser: Dr. Linda D. Labbo, Department of Reading Education, College of Education, The University of Georgia

COMPASS POINT BOOKS ✦ MINNEAPOLIS, MINNESOTA

Compass Point Books
3109 West 50th Street, #115
Minneapolis, MN 55410

Visit Compass Point Books on the Internet at *www.compasspointbooks.com*
or e-mail your request to *custserv@compasspointbooks.com*

Photographs ©: White House Collection, Courtesy White House Historical Association (45), cover, 3;
Rutherford B. Hayes Presidential Center, Fremont, Ohio, 6, 10, 11, 12, 13, 14, 16, 17 (top), 19, 25, 33,
37, 43, 44, 47, 48, 49, 50, 55 (left, all), 56 (bottom left), 57 (left); Library of Congress, 7, 18, 21, 35,
40, 56 (top right), 58 (top left), 59 (left, all); Hulton/Archive by Getty Images, 8, 17 (bottom), 26, 31,
42, 54 (right), 55 (bottom right), 59 (right); Corbis, 9, 20, 27, 30, 32, 54 (left), 56 (bottom right);
Lombard Antiquarian Maps & Prints, 15, 41, 56 (top left); Kelly-Mooney Photography/Corbis, 22;
Ohio State University Archives, 23; National Portrait Gallery, Smithsonian Institution/Art Resource,
N.Y., 24; Bettmann/Corbis, 28, 38; Stock Montage, 29; Image Courtesy of the Currency Gallery, 45,
58 (bottom left); Texas State Library & Archives Commission, 55 (top right); Union Pacific Museum
Collection, 57 (right); Denver Public Library, Western History Collection, 58 (right).

Editors: E. Russell Primm, Emily J. Dolbear, Melissa McDaniel, and Catherine Neitge
Photo Researcher: Svetlana Zhurkina
Photo Selector: Linda S. Koutris
Designer/Page Production: The Design Lab/Les Tranby
Cartographer: XNR Productions, Inc.

Library of Congress Cataloging-in-Publication Data
   Rutherford B. Hayes / by Andrew Santella.
      p. cm. — (Profiles of the presidents)
Summary: A biography of the nineteenth president of the United States,
discussing his personal life, education, and political career.
Includes bibliographical references (p.) and index.
   ISBN 0-7565-0266-7 (alk. paper)
   1. Hayes, Rutherford Birchard, 1822–1893—Juvenile literature. 2. Presidents—United States—
Biography—Juvenile literature. [1. Hayes, Rutherford Birchard, 1822–1893. 2. Presidents.] I. Title. II. Series.
   E682 .S26 2003
   973.8'3'092—dc21   2002153521

Table of Contents

★ ★ ★

*NOTE: In this book, words that are defined in the glossary are in **bold** the first time they appear in the text.*

The Warrior Politician

★ ★ ★

Colonel Rutherford B. Hayes was too busy for politics. His friends wanted him to **campaign** in the 1864 election for the U.S. Congress, but Hayes had more pressing business.

Rutherford B. Hayes in his army uniform in 1861

The Civil War (1861–1865) between the Northern and Southern states was in its third year. Hayes was leading his men in heavy fighting against Southern troops in Virginia, and it was no time for him to be thinking about politics. "An officer who would leave the army at this time to electioneer for a seat in Congress ought to be scalped," Hayes told his friends.

So Hayes stayed with his troops. On October 19, 1864, he led them into battle at Cedar Creek, Virginia. The fighting was intense. The horse Hayes was riding was killed by gunfire. Hayes was thrown to the ground and knocked unconscious. Some of his men feared he was dead, but Hayes soon recovered and rejoined his troops. His men cheered when they learned he was safe. One soldier called Hayes "a lion of a leader."

▲ *The battle at Cedar Creek in 1864*

While Hayes was camped with his troops in Virginia, he learned that he had been elected to Congress. Though Hayes had refused to campaign, he had easily won the election. His bravery in battle had made him a war hero, and that helped him become a congressman. His term of office officially began in January 1865. Hayes, however, did not leave the army until the summer of 1865, after the war was over.

This 1878 ▼ illustration shows President Hayes trying to reunite the North and South after the Civil War.

One of Hayes's first jobs as a congressman was to help bring the divided country back together after the terrible destruction of the Civil War. More than ten years after the war's end, Hayes was still working at that challenge—as president of the United States.

Preparing for Greatness

★ ★ ★

No one expected Rutherford B. Hayes to survive his first few years of life, let alone become president of the United States. Hayes was born on October 4, 1822, in Delaware, Ohio. As a baby, he was so sick and weak that his mother and the family doctors feared he might not live long. Luckily, young Rutherford somehow survived these difficult years.

◄ The house where Rutherford B. Hayes was born in Delaware, Ohio

Rutherford's ▶
mother, Sophia
Birchard Hayes

He was named for his father, Rutherford Hayes. However, father and son would never get to know one another. The elder Hayes collapsed and died while working on the family farm ten weeks before his son was born. Little Rutherford Birchard Hayes grew up as the only male in the Hayes home. His mother, Sophia, and his older sister, Fanny, cared for him. They nicknamed him Rud, or Ruddy.

◄ *Fanny Hayes encouraged her younger brother to grow up to be someone important.*

Sophia taught her son to read and write, and Fanny took Ruddy along when she walked in the woods near the family farm. Fanny insisted that her little brother would grow up to be someone important. She encouraged him to aim for greatness. Soon he was memorizing speeches from American history and repeating them for the neighbors.

Sardis Birchard ▶
helped pay for
Ruddy's education.

      Sardis Birchard was Ruddy's uncle and another great influence on his life. Birchard often visited the Hayes family and helped pay for the boy's education, making sure Ruddy attended the best schools available. Ruddy left home at fourteen to attend Norwalk Academy in Norwalk, Ohio. The following year, he traveled even farther from home to take classes at a school in Middletown, Connecticut.

With his uncle's help, Hayes was next admitted to Kenyon College in Gambier, Ohio. He quickly made friends there and did well in his studies. One school report praised his "strength of mind" and "soundness of judgment." When Hayes graduated from Kenyon in 1842, he was selected to give a speech at the ceremony.

Birchard urged his nephew to continue studying and to eventually become a lawyer. Young Hayes agreed. He spent a year learning the basics of law while working for a lawyer in Columbus, Ohio. Then he headed to Harvard Law School in Massachusetts for more formal legal training. Hayes completed his law degree in 1845.

▼ *Hayes (left) and two classmates at Kenyon College*

*Rutherford B. Hayes ▶
at age twenty-four*

Hayes set up his law office in his uncle's hometown of Lower Sandusky, Ohio. Lower Sandusky was a small, quiet area. Hayes spent nearly five years there, slowly building his legal practice. However, he eventually grew tired of the slow pace of life in the little town and decided to make a change. In 1849, Hayes moved to Cincinnati, Ohio, vowing to become a successful lawyer in the big city.

A Rising Star

★ ★ ★

Cincinnati was growing rapidly when Hayes arrived there. He enjoyed the excitement of its busy streets. He eagerly joined clubs and went to plays and lectures. Hayes also began attending parties with Lucy Ware Webb, an old friend from Delaware, Ohio. Lucy was a student at Wesleyan Female College in Cincinnati. She and Hayes soon fell in love.

◄ Cincinnati, Ohio, during the 1850s

Rutherford B. ▶ Hayes and Lucy Ware Webb on their wedding day, December 30, 1852

Lucy Webb was the daughter of a wealthy and politically active Ohio family. She was well educated and had strong opinions that she was not afraid to voice, including her belief that slavery was terribly wrong. At that time, slavery was banned in the Northern states but allowed in the Southern states. Lucy was an **abolitionist** who believed it should be outlawed everywhere. She also thought that women should play a bigger role in political life. Lucy's interest in politics helped shape Hayes's own political beliefs.

In 1852, the two were married. During the years to come, Lucy gave birth to seven sons and one daughter, though only five of the children lived to adulthood.

At Lucy's urging, Hayes became active in the fight to end slavery. He sometimes served as a lawyer for runaway slaves and the abolitionists who helped them. He also assisted the movement called the Underground Railroad, which gave aid to runaway slaves escaping to the North. In 1856, Hayes joined the new Republican Party, which was committed to stopping the spread of slavery.

▲ *Lucy Hayes holding the Hayes's oldest child, Birchard, in 1854*

◄ *Abolitionists standing outside an Ohio jail where they rescued a runaway slave*

Hayes became known in Cincinnati political circles, and he soon had the chance to hold his first public office. In 1858, he was appointed city attorney for Cincinnati. The following year, he was elected to the same position by voters. However, Hayes's budding career was about to be interrupted by war.

As the 1860s began, the issue of slavery was splitting the United States apart. The Republican Party wanted to stop slavery from spreading into new U.S. territories in the West. Northern abolitionists wanted to outlaw slavery completely. Southern slave owners, on the other hand,

The opening battle ▸
of the Civil War
occurred at Fort
Sumter, South
Carolina, on
April 12, 1861.

defended their right to own slaves. They were alarmed by the election of Republican Abraham Lincoln to the presidency in 1860. They feared that Lincoln would put an end to slavery in the South. Eleven Southern states refused to accept Lincoln as their president. Instead, they announced that they would withdraw from the Union. In 1861, Northern and Southern states went to war.

▲ Like her husband, Lucy Hayes also became involved in the war effort. Here she is shown visiting wounded soliders at a Union hospital.

Lincoln called for men to sign up to fight to save the Union. Rutherford B. Hayes answered the call. Hayes was thirty-eight years old and the father of three young boys. Still, he insisted on joining the battle. He told a friend he would rather die fighting for his country than "live through the war without taking any part in it."

Hayes began his military career as a major and quickly won the respect of his men. One of them was a private named William McKinley, who would also one day become president of the United States. Again and again, Hayes proved his bravery in battle. He was wounded four times during the four years he fought in the war. He rose to the rank of major general and was praised for his "gallant and distinguished service."

Future presidents ▼ Rutherford B. Hayes (immediately left of monument) and William McKinley (second to right of monument) standing next to a war memorial dedicated to their army unit in Cleveland, Ohio, in 1865

News of Hayes's bravery on the battlefield spread to his home state of Ohio. His conduct made him such a hero in Ohio that he easily won election to the U.S. Congress in 1864. By that time, it was becoming clear that the North would win the Civil War. The next challenge would be to bring North and South together again as one united nation.

▲ *President Abraham Lincoln was shot and killed in April 1865.*

Many Northerners believed that the Southern states should be punished for breaking away from the Union. Then, in 1865, a Southerner shot and killed President Lincoln. This made even more Northerners want to take revenge on the South.

The main reading ▲ room at the Library of Congress in Washington, D.C.

Shortly after the end of the Civil War, the Republican Party enacted policies called **Reconstruction.** The aim of Reconstruction was to rebuild the war-damaged South and to protect the rights of former slaves so they could live and vote as free people. To do this, the U.S. government stationed troops in several parts of the South. In Congress, Hayes supported Reconstruction by voting for laws that helped ensure fair elections in the South. He also used his influence in Congress to pass laws that helped turn the Library of Congress into a true national library.

★

Hayes never felt at home in Washington. He missed Lucy and his family, and he disliked the constant arguing in Congress. In 1867, he returned to Ohio, where he was elected governor. As governor, he pushed to improve conditions in Ohio's hospitals, prisons, and schools. Hayes said that his proudest accomplishment as governor was helping to establish Ohio State University. For the rest of his life, he would work to improve American education.

▾ *Hayes Hall, which was built in the 1890s, is located on the campus of Ohio State University. It is named after Rutherford B. Hayes, who helped establish the college.*

Ulysses S. Grant ▲
was president from
1869 to 1877.

It was a tradition in Ohio that no governor served more than two terms in a row. So after completing his second term as governor in 1872, Hayes retired to Cincinnati. Then he made another run for Congress. Many voters, however, were angry about Reconstruction. While Republican Ulysses S. Grant was president, government agencies involved in Reconstruction were filled with **corrupt** and dishonest workers. Voters responded by voting against Republicans, and Hayes lost the election. After his defeat, he moved to Fremont, Ohio. He lived in a home called Spiegel Grove, which his Uncle Sardis had given him.

Hayes was known as an honest and fair man. Ohio Republicans believed that he was exactly what their party needed to win back the approval of voters. In 1875, Republican leaders convinced Hayes to run for governor for a third time. He won, and his election made national news. Suddenly, people all over the country were saying that Hayes was ready to move on to bigger and better things. Hayes knew it, too. He wrote in his diary, "I am likely to be pushed for the Republican nomination for President."

▲ When Hayes was elected governor of Ohio for a third time in 1875, it made national news.

"His Fraudulency"

★　★　★

Republicans had been in the White House since 1861. Party leaders knew, however, that it would be a challenge to win the presidency again in 1876. Democrats were sure to remind voters about the corrupt government workers who played a role in Grant's presidency. For the Republicans to win, they would have to beat back charges of crooked politics. As a result, they needed a **candidate** known for his honesty. Many Republicans looked to Rutherford B. Hayes.

James G. Blaine hoped to run as the Republican candidate in the presidential election of 1876.

Hayes made an excellent candidate for president. Besides being honest and well respected, he was a war hero. In addition, he came from Ohio, a state with a large population. Republicans hoped that Hayes's popularity in Ohio would help them win votes there. However, Congressman James G. Blaine of Maine was also in the running to become the Republican candidate for president.

◄ *Republican running mates Rutherford B. Hayes (left) and William Wheeler*

In 1876, the Republican Party held its **convention** to select a presidential candidate in Cincinnati. When the convention started, Blaine had more support than Hayes. That quickly changed, however. Because the convention was in Ohio, crowds of local Hayes supporters attended. They wore Hayes buttons and cheered loudly, helping rally support for the native Ohioan. Finally, Republican leaders settled on Hayes as their choice for president. New York congressman William Wheeler would be the Republican candidate for vice president. "Hurrah for Hayes and honest ways!" said Republicans across the country.

The Democratic candidate was Governor Samuel Tilden of New York. Like Hayes, Tilden was known for his honesty and clean politics. Tilden had fought to rid New York City of corrupt politicians and hoped to bring clean politics to the White House, as well. He claimed that Reconstruction was only helping dishonest politicians and businessmen make money. Tilden called for an end to Republican rule and Reconstruction. "Throw the rascals out," said Tilden's supporters.

The election of 1876 turned out to be one of the closest in American history. In the days leading up to

A campaign poster supporting Tilden in the 1876 election

▲ Campaign headquarters for Hayes's supporters in San Francisco, California

the election, no one could tell who would win. As the votes began to come in, Tilden seemed to have an edge. On election night, Hayes went to bed thinking he had lost. When he woke up the next morning, he learned that votes were still being counted. The election was too close to call.

Samuel Tilden won ▲
more popular votes
than Hayes.

In fact, the election would not be decided for months. It was clear that Tilden had won more votes than Hayes. However, the president of the United States is not elected by a simple count of the votes. Instead, a complicated system involving the electoral college decides who will be president. In this system, each state is given a certain number of electoral college votes based on its population. Whoever wins the most votes in a state wins all of that state's electoral college votes. The candidate who wins the most electoral college votes becomes president. This means it is possible for a candidate to win the election even if he does not receive the largest number of popular votes.

The election of 1876 came down to a few states. Both Republicans and Democrats claimed victory in Florida, Oregon, South Carolina, and Louisiana. Each side accused the other of cheating. To resolve the dispute, Congress appointed a special commission. It was made up of five U.S. senators, five members of the U.S. House of Representatives, and five justices from the U.S. Supreme Court. Of the ten elected officials who served on the commission, five were Republicans, and five were Democrats.

▼ A meeting of the special commission appointed to resolve the dispute over electoral college votes in the 1876 election

Democrats claimed that the Republicans were stealing the election. One congressman threatened to lead thousands of Democrats on a march to Washington to see that Tilden was made president. Tilden called for calm. "It will not do to fight," he said. "We have just emerged from one civil war, and it will never do to engage in another."

Meanwhile, Democratic and Republican leaders searched for a solution. Republicans promised that if Hayes were declared the winner, he would withdraw federal troops from Louisiana and South Carolina. This would mean the end to Reconstruction, which was what the Democrats wanted. The two sides struck a deal, and the commission declared Hayes

A torchlight parade ▶
in honor of Hayes's
inauguration

the winner. Congress made the decision official on March 2, 1877, just three days before the new president was to be sworn into office.

The inauguration of President Hayes on March 5, 1877

On March 5, 1877, a crowd of more than thirty thousand people watched Rutherford B. Hayes take the oath of office as the nineteenth president of the United States. In fact, Hayes had already taken the oath. Because **inauguration** day fell on a Sunday in 1877, the event was put off until Monday. Rather than wait to become president, Hayes took the oath of office in private on Saturday, March 3. Two days later, he repeated the oath for the crowd.

In his inauguration speech, Hayes aimed to calm a nation that had been shaken by the election. He promised to work to improve the way presidents were elected. He said he would try to heal the divide between North and South. Hayes also urged both the Democratic and the Republican Parties to stop feuding. He told his audience that serving the nation was more important than fighting for a particular political party. "He serves his party best who serves his country best," Hayes declared.

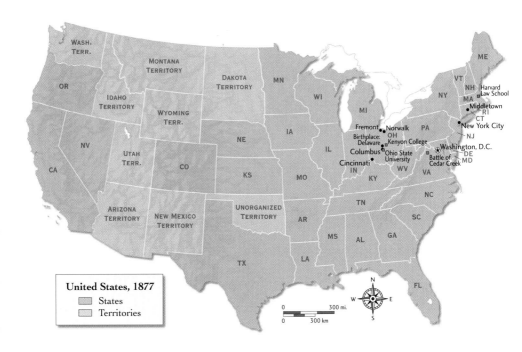

Hayes's critics were not convinced by his speech. As they saw it, Hayes did not deserve to be president. They claimed he was elected through fraud, or cheating. Some gave Hayes nicknames like Ruther-fraud or His Fraudulency. Certain Democratic congressmen even refused to attend the inauguration.

▲ *Democrat David Key became Hayes's postmaster general.*

Hayes wanted to be fair to Democrats and Republicans, and he was determined to represent both North and South. He kept this in mind when the time came to appoint members of his **cabinet.** Hayes chose people from various parts of the country and picked politicians who had different political beliefs. He even took the unusual step of naming someone from an opposing political party to his cabinet. Democrat David Key became postmaster general.

The End of Reconstruction

★ ★ ★

During the election dispute, Hayes's supporters had promised that he would end Republican Reconstruction policies if chosen as president. One month into his presidency, Hayes kept that promise. He believed that Reconstruction was breeding hatred among Southerners and was keeping the nation divided.

Under Reconstruction, federal troops had been sent to certain parts of the South. Their job was to protect the rights of African-Americans and state governments. Southerners resented the presence of these troops, so Hayes ordered that they return to their barracks. He reasoned that this was the only way the South's government would ever return to normal. "My policy is trust, peace, and put aside the **bayonet**," Hayes said.

◄ A photo of
Rutherford B. Hayes
taken shortly after
he was elected
president

Hayes called for spending federal money to rebuild the war-torn South. He believed that new roads and railroads should be built to help the Southern economy. Hayes also pledged support for free education, which he said was the key to a strong economy in the South.

An African-American passenger leaves the "colored" waiting room at the bus terminal in Jackson, Mississippi, in 1961. One hundred years after the Civil War, blacks in the South still did not have equal rights.

The end of Reconstruction was not good for everyone in the South. It was a disaster for African-Americans. Without the protection of federal troops, white Southerners took away their most basic rights. Many African-Americans were denied their right to vote. As a result, black elected officials were voted out of office. State after state in the South passed laws separating blacks and whites. Blacks were not allowed to go to the same schools or sit in the same train cars as whites. It would be nearly one hundred years before African-Americans in the South again enjoyed basic rights.

Democrats soon took control of politics in the entire region. Though Samuel Tilden had lost the election of 1876, the end of Reconstruction proved to be a huge victory for southern Democrats.

Bringing Change to Washington

★　★　★

In his inauguration speech, Hayes had promised honest and fair government. He quickly set about proving to the nation that he meant to keep his promise. Hayes began by attacking what was known as the spoils system. In the spoils system, elected officials gave government jobs to

People seeking government positions crowd the White House shortly after Hayes's inauguration.

supporters as a reward for helping them win an election. Often, these people were not prepared to do the jobs that had been awarded to them. Worse yet, some employees earning good salaries did little work because they knew they did not have to worry about losing their jobs. In short, the spoils system produced dishonest and lazy government.

▲ *Chester A. Arthur, who would later become U.S. president, was fired by Hayes in 1878 as supervisor of the Port of New York.*

Hayes wanted to end the spoils system. He insisted that government jobs should be given only to people who proved they were skilled workers. Hayes wanted federal employees to be chosen without regard to their political party. In 1877, he signed an order forbidding federal workers from taking an active part in political campaigns. Hayes even fired the supervisor of the Port of New York for not stopping his workers from being corrupt. The supervisor's name was Chester A. Arthur, and he would later become president of the United States.

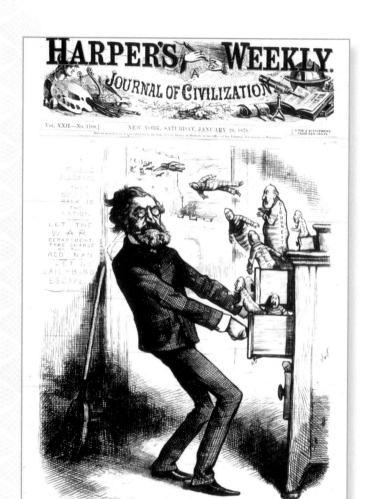

An 1878 political cartoon showing Secretary of the Interior Carl Schurz investigating corruption within the Bureau of Indian Affairs

Hayes also attempted to bring changes to the government's Bureau of Indian Affairs. The bureau was in charge of lands set aside for Native Americans. Hayes tried to improve life for Native Americans, but many Indians continued to suffer at the hands of corrupt government officials.

While Hayes was trying to clean up government, his wife was earning the respect of the American people. Lucy Hayes became the first wife of a president to be called the first lady, after a magazine article gave her that title. More importantly, she was the first wife of a president to have graduated from college. She spoke out on political issues more freely than most women of her time. Lucy urged her husband to support women's rights and believed it was important for women to be well educated.

◄ *Lucy and Rutherford B. Hayes in 1877*

Lucy Hayes also made her dislike of alcohol well known. Because of her opinions and for political considerations, President Hayes decided not to serve alcohol at White House parties. Though this decision was not popular with some people in Washington, Hayes stood by it. The practice later earned Mrs. Hayes the nickname Lemonade Lucy.

Lucy Hayes at the White House with her daughter Fanny (right), son Scott, and Carrie Davis, daughter of artist Theodore Davis, who created the Hayes's White House china

The Civil War had been expensive. To pay for it, the U.S. government printed paper money called greenbacks. However, the government did not have enough gold to back up the greenbacks. That meant that if people were allowed to trade in the greenbacks for gold, the government would not be able to pay for them all. As a result, Americans did not trust the paper money, and it lost value. A one dollar greenback was no longer worth the same as a silver dollar coin or a dollar in gold. By the time Hayes became president in 1877, the situation with the greenbacks was hurting the American economy.

▲ *A one dollar bill from 1878*

President Hayes worked to repair the economy. The government increased its supply of gold. By 1879, a one dollar bill was again worth one dollar in gold. The government was also able to pay off the last of its debts from the Civil War.

Meanwhile, the nation's largest railroads were losing so much money that they cut their workers' pay. This caused the railroad employees to go on **strike.** Rather than pay the workers more, the railroads simply hired new people. In several states, strikers reacted by attacking these new workers. They set fire to trains and destroyed tracks, doing millions of dollars worth of damage. Dozens of people died in the riots.

Hayes took a middle approach to the strike. He sent in federal troops, but only when local officials asked for them. He did not break the strike, though many workers believed he was on the side of the railroad companies. In time, the workers gave in, and the strike came to an end.

After the Presidency

★   ★   ★

While running for president, Hayes had pledged to serve just one term if elected. As the election of 1880 approached, he held fast to his promise. Hayes watched from the sidelines as the Republican Party chose James A.

◄ *President and Mrs. Hayes in Yosemite, California, during a tour of the West in 1880*

Garfield as their candidate for president. He was pleased when Garfield defeated Democrat Winfield S. Hancock and kept the Republican Party in the White House. However, Hayes was even more pleased to be leaving the presidency. "Nobody ever left the presidency with less regret," he said.

Hayes did not retire from public life, though. After leaving Washington in 1881, he continued working for a number of his favorite causes. He devoted himself to improving public education and supporting colleges. Hayes also enjoyed having more time to spend with Lucy at their home, Spiegel Grove.

Former president ▶
Hayes and Mrs.
Hayes (center) with
their children (from
left) Birchard (with
his wife, Mary),
Scott, Rutherford,
Fanny, and Webb
on the porch of
Spiegel Grove

◀ *Hayes with (from left) his son Rutherford, family friend Lucy Herron, and his daughter Fanny in 1889, shortly after the death of his wife*

Hayes was deeply saddened when Lucy died in 1889. For the rest of his life, he traveled with framed pictures of her. To keep his mind off his loss, he stayed busy. "I am shoving on to the end," he wrote a friend.

Rutherford Hayes became seriously ill with heart trouble during one of his many trips. Knowing that he might not live long, he insisted on returning to Spiegel Grove. He died there on January 17, 1893. His last words were, "I know I am going where Lucy is."

Grover Cleveland, who would soon be sworn in as president, attended Hayes's funeral, along with Ohio governor William McKinley. Some of the men who had fought under Hayes in the Civil War lined up to pay their last respects to their commander. They remembered him as a brave officer. The rest of the nation remembered him as the president who led the nation in healing the wounds left by the Civil War.

The funeral ▼ procession of Rutherford B. Hayes in Fremont, Ohio, in 1893

GLOSSARY

★ ★ ★

abolitionist—someone who supported the banning of slavery

bayonet—a blade attached to the end of a rifle

cabinet—a president's group of advisers who are heads of government departments

campaign—an organized effort to win an election

candidate—someone running for office in an election

convention—a large meeting during which a political party chooses its candidates

corrupt—willing to break laws to get money or power

inauguration—a president's swearing-in ceremony

Reconstruction—the system for bringing the Southern states back into the United States after the Civil War

strike—when workers refuse to work, hoping to force their company to agree to their demands

RUTHERFORD B. HAYES'S LIFE AT A GLANCE

★ ★ ★

PERSONAL

Nickname:	Ruther-fraud, His Fraudulency
Born:	October 4, 1822
Birthplace:	Delaware, Ohio
Father's name:	Rutherford Hayes
Mother's name:	Sophia Birchard Hayes
Education:	Graduated from Kenyon College in 1842 and from Harvard Law School in 1845
Wife's name:	Lucy Ware Webb Hayes (1831–1889)
Married:	December 30, 1852
Children:	Birchard Austin Hayes (1853–1926); James Webb Cook Hayes (1856–1934); Rutherford Platt Hayes (1858–1927); Joseph Thompson Hayes (1861–1863); George Crook Hayes (1864–1866); Fanny Hayes (1867–1950); Scott Russell Hayes (1871–1923); Manning Force Hayes (1873–1874)
Died:	January 17, 1893, in Fremont, Ohio
Buried:	Spiegel Grove in Fremont, Ohio

PUBLIC

Occupation before presidency:	Lawyer, public official
Occupation after presidency:	None
Military service:	Major general in the Union army in the Civil War
Other government positions:	Member of the U.S. House of Representatives from Ohio; governor of Ohio
Political party:	Republican
Vice president:	William A. Wheeler (1877–1881)
Dates in office:	March 4, 1877–March 4, 1881
Presidential opponent:	Samuel J. Tilden (Democrat), 1876
Number of votes (Electoral College):	4,036,572 of 8,320,592 (185 of 369), 1876
Writings:	*Diary and Letters,* 5 vols. (1922–1926)

★

Rutherford B. Hayes's Cabinet

Secretary of state:
  William M. Evarts (1877–1881)

Secretary of the treasury:
  John Sherman (1877–1881)

Secretary of war:
  George W. McCrary (1877–1879)
  Alexander Ramsey (1879–1881)

Attorney general:
  Charles Devens (1877–1881)

Postmaster general:
  David M. Key (1877–1880)
  Horace Maynard (1880–1881)

Secretary of the navy:
  Richard W. Thompson (1877–1880)
  Nathan Goff Jr. (1881)

Secretary of the interior:
  Carl Schurz (1877–1881)

RUTHERFORD B. HAYES'S LIFE AND TIMES

★ ★ ★

HAYES'S LIFE

October 4, Hayes is born in Delaware, Ohio (below) — 1822

1820

WORLD EVENTS

1823 — Mexico becomes a republic

1826 — The first photograph is taken by Joseph Niépce, a French physicist

1827 — Modern-day matches are invented by coating the end of a wooden stick with phosphorus

1829 — The first practical sewing machine is invented by French tailor Barthélemy Thimonnier (above)

HAYES'S LIFE

WORLD EVENTS

1830

1833   Great Britain
        abolishes slavery

1836   Texans defeat Mexican
        troops at San Jacinto after
        a deadly battle at the
        Alamo (below)

1837   American banker J. P.
        Morgan is born

Graduates from   1842
Kenyon College

1840   1840   Auguste Rodin, famous
                    sculptor of *The Thinker*,
                    is born

Graduates from   1845
Harvard Law School

1848   *The Communist Manifesto,*
        by German writer Karl
        Marx (above), is widely
        distributed

HAYES'S LIFE

Opens a law office in   1849
Cincinnati, Ohio (below)

Marries Lucy   1852
Ware Webb

Becomes the Cincinnati   1858
city attorney

Joins the Union army   1861

Elected to the U.S.   1864
House of Representatives

WORLD EVENTS

1850

1852   American Harriet Beecher
Stowe (above) publishes
Uncle Tom's Cabin

1858   English scientist Charles
Darwin (below) presents
his theory of evolution

1860   1860   Austrian composer Gustav
Mahler is born in Kalischt
(now in Austria)

1865   Lewis Carroll writes *Alice's
Adventures in Wonderland*

HAYES'S LIFE

Elected governor of Ohio   1867

Runs for Congress and loses   1872

Elected governor of   1875
Ohio for a third time

WORLD EVENTS

1867   U.S. buys Alaska from
Russia for $7.2 million

1868   Louisa May Alcott
publishes *Little Women*

1869   The periodic table of
elements is invented

The transcontinental
railroad across the United
States is completed (below)

1870   John D. Rockefeller founds
the Standard Oil Company

1873   Typewriters get the
QWERTY keyboard

1875   Thomas Edison invents
the mimeograph

1870

HAYES'S LIFE

Presidential Election Results:		Popular Votes	Electoral Votes
1876	Rutherford B. Hayes	4,036,572	185
	Samuel J. Tilden	4,284,020	184

April, federal troops are withdrawn from South Carolina and Louisiana — 1877

June, Hayes signs an order barring federal workers from taking part in political campaigns

Fires Chester A. Arthur as supervisor of the Port of New York — 1878

Greenbacks (below) return to their full value — 1879

WORLD EVENTS

1876 The Battle of the Little Bighorn is a victory for Native Americans defending their homes in the West against General George Custer (below)

Alexander Graham Bell uses the first telephone to speak to his assistant, Thomas Watson

1877 German inventor Nikolaus A. Otto works on what will become the internal combustion engine for automobiles

Tchaikovsky composes his famous ballet *Swan Lake*.

1879 Electric lights are invented

HAYES'S LIFE

First Easter egg roll on the   1880
White House lawn

Becomes the first president
to visit the West Coast
while in office (below)

January 17, dies of   1893
heart trouble

WORLD EVENTS

1880

1882   Thomas Edison builds
a power station

1884   Mark Twain (above)
publishes *The Adventures
of Huckleberry Finn*

1886   Grover Cleveland
dedicates the Statue of
Liberty in New York

Bombing in Haymarket
Square, Chicago, due to
labor unrest

1890

1891   The Roman Catholic
Church publishes the
encyclical *Rerum Novarum,*
which supports the rights
of labor

1893   Women gain voting
privileges in New Zealand,
the first country to take
such a step

UNDERSTANDING RUTHERFORD B. HAYES AND HIS PRESIDENCY

★ ★ ★

IN THE LIBRARY

Francis, Sandra. *Rutherford B. Hayes: Our 19th President.*
Chanhassen, Minn.: The Child's World, 2001.

Kent, Zachary. *Rutherford B. Hayes: Nineteenth President of the United States.*
Chicago: Children's Press, 1989.

Welsbacher, Anne. *Rutherford B. Hayes.* Edina, Minn.:
Abdo & Daughters, 2001.

ON THE WEB

The Rutherford B. Hayes Presidential Center
http://www.rbhayes.org/default.htm
To learn more about the life and presidency of Hayes

The American President—Rutherford B. Hayes
http://www.americanpresident.org/history/rutherfordbhayes
For in-depth information about Hayes and his presidency

Internet Public Library—Rutherford B. Hayes
http://www.ipl.org/div/potus/rbhayes.html
For information about Hayes's presidency
and many links to other resources

HAYES HISTORIC SITES
ACROSS THE COUNTRY

Rutherford B. Hayes Presidential Center
Spiegel Grove
Fremont, OH 43420
419/332-2081
To visit Hayes's home and a museum
dedicated to his life and presidency

Rutherford B. Hayes Birthplace
East William Street
Delaware, OH 43015
To see where Hayes was born

Cedar Creek Battlefield
8437 Valley Pike
Middletown, VA 22645
540/869-2064
To visit the Civil War battlefield
where Hayes was wounded

THE U.S. PRESIDENTS
(Years in Office)

★ ★ ★

1. **George Washington**
   (March 4, 1789–March 3, 1797)
2. **John Adams**
   (March 4, 1797–March 3, 1801)
3. **Thomas Jefferson**
   (March 4, 1801–March 3, 1809)
4. **James Madison**
   (March 4, 1809–March 3, 1817)
5. **James Monroe**
   (March 4, 1817–March 3, 1825)
6. **John Quincy Adams**
   (March 4, 1825–March 3, 1829)
7. **Andrew Jackson**
   (March 4, 1829–March 3, 1837)
8. **Martin Van Buren**
   (March 4, 1837–March 3, 1841)
9. **William Henry Harrison**
   (March 6, 1841–April 4, 1841)
10. **John Tyler**
    (April 6, 1841–March 3, 1845)
11. **James K. Polk**
    (March 4, 1845–March 3, 1849)
12. **Zachary Taylor**
    (March 5, 1849–July 9, 1850)
13. **Millard Fillmore**
    (July 10, 1850–March 3, 1853)
14. **Franklin Pierce**
    (March 4, 1853–March 3, 1857)
15. **James Buchanan**
    (March 4, 1857–March 3, 1861)
16. **Abraham Lincoln**
    (March 4, 1861–April 15, 1865)
17. **Andrew Johnson**
    (April 15, 1865–March 3, 1869)
18. **Ulysses S. Grant**
    (March 4, 1869–March 3, 1877)
19. Rutherford B. Hayes
    (March 4, 1877–March 3, 1881)
20. **James Garfield**
    (March 4, 1881–Sept 19, 1881)
21. **Chester Arthur**
    (Sept 20, 1881–March 3, 1885)
22. **Grover Cleveland**
    (March 4, 1885–March 3, 1889)
23. **Benjamin Harrison**
    (March 4, 1889–March 3, 1893)
24. **Grover Cleveland**
    (March 4, 1893–March 3, 1897)
25. **William McKinley**
    (March 4, 1897–September 14, 1901)
26. **Theodore Roosevelt**
    (September 14, 1901–March 3, 1909)
27. **William Howard Taft**
    (March 4, 1909–March 3, 1913)
28. **Woodrow Wilson**
    (March 4, 1913–March 3, 1921)
29. **Warren G. Harding**
    (March 4, 1921–August 2, 1923)
30. **Calvin Coolidge**
    (August 3, 1923–March 3, 1929)
31. **Herbert Hoover**
    (March 4, 1929–March 3, 1933)
32. **Franklin D. Roosevelt**
    (March 4, 1933–April 12, 1945)
33. **Harry S. Truman**
    (April 12, 1945–January 20, 1953)
34. **Dwight D. Eisenhower**
    (January 20, 1953–January 20, 1961)
35. **John F. Kennedy**
    (January 20, 1961–November 22, 1963)
36. **Lyndon B. Johnson**
    (November 22, 1963–January 20, 1969)
37. **Richard M. Nixon**
    (January 20, 1969–August 9, 1974)
38. **Gerald R. Ford**
    (August 9, 1974–January 20, 1977)
39. **James Earl Carter**
    (January 20, 1977–January 20, 1981)
40. **Ronald Reagan**
    (January 20, 1981–January 20, 1989)
41. **George H. W. Bush**
    (January 20, 1989–January 20, 1993)
42. **William Jefferson Clinton**
    (January 20, 1993–January 20, 2001)
43. **George W. Bush**
    (January 20, 2001–)

INDEX

★ ★ ★

ABOUT THE AUTHOR

Andrew Santella writes for magazines and newspapers, including *GQ* and the *New York Times Book Review.* He is the author of a number of books for young readers. He lives outside Chicago, with his wife and son.